Dear Students,

Skilled writers often use other writers' work to inform their own. Sometimes they quote from other works, or sources, directly, and sometimes the other works provide information that they paraphrase or summarize. In either case, writers must always identify their sources when they include other writers' ideas or research.

Professional organizations like the Modern Language Association (MLA) and the American Psychological Association (APA) publish reference manuals that provide specific guidelines on how to cite your sources. In your textbook, you'll find models for how to identify researched material within a paper as well as how to list all of the sources you have used in a single writing assignment.

From time to time, both the MLA and APA revise their manuals to reflect changes in the sources that are available to researchers or the thinking behind how best to cite them. These revisions may include new kinds of sources (like blogs or tweets) or new ways of identifying both digital and print sources. In April 2016, the Modern Language Association published a revised version of its handbook; the eighth edition of the *MLA Handbook* includes many changes to its recommended practices for citing sources.

The editors at McGraw-Hill Education are currently updating all of our textbooks and online materials to reflect these changes to the *MLA Handbook*. However, that process takes some time, and we want to supply our customers with these changes as soon as possible. Therefore, we have published this small booklet as an aid to both students and instructors in composition courses. The booklet is free of charge to anyone who has purchased a new copy of a McGraw-Hill composition textbook that has not already been updated.

Our booklet includes new guidelines and models based on the 2016 *MLA Handbook*, 8th edition. **You can find a directory to the different types of in-text citations and works-cited entries on pp. 30-32 of this booklet.** Students and instructors may elect to use this booklet in place of the chapter or chapters on MLA style contained within your textbook. Ask your instructor which version he or she prefers that you use for your assignments.

With all best wishes,

The Editors

1

MLA Style for In-Text Citations

The information you provide in parenthetical citations depends on the way you incorporate, or place, researched materials into your paper. There are a number of ways to do this using MLA formats. The formats given here are found in the eighth edition of the *MLA Handbook* (MLA, 2016). If your instructor asks you to use American Psychological Association (APA) or *Chicago Manual of Style* (CMS) formats, consult the relevant chapters in your textbook or the current editions of the *Publication Manual of the American Psychological Association* or *The Chicago Manual of Style*.

1. SUMMARIZED OR PARAPHRASED MATERIAL Remember that you must cite the source of material that you summarize and paraphrase, as well as the source of material that you quote. Often the easiest way to cite your source is to put the last name of the author and the page number of the source in parentheses after the summarized or paraphrased material. In the following example, Charles Da Rienzo, a student who wrote a paper about identity theft, summarizes information from page 73 of a book by Paul Bocij.

> Companies use spyware to steal industrial secrets from competitors, but individuals can also use spyware. For instance, husbands and wives who have suspicions about their mates have been known to keep track of them by using this software (Bocij 73).

Note that no punctuation separates the author's last name and the page number nor is the abbreviation *p*. (for "page") used. The period that ends the sentence appears after the closing parenthesis.

2. DIRECT QUOTATION WITH THE AUTHOR'S LAST NAME IN THE TEXT OF YOUR PAPER Often it is a good idea to name the author of the direct quotation in your text. In the following example, the student directly quotes a sentence from an article by Frank Abagnale and introduces it with a **signal phrase**, which includes the author's name and a verb such as *argues*, *claims*, or *has written*. Because the quotation is a complete sentence, the student has chosen to set it off from her own writing with a colon. And because the student uses the author's name to introduce the quotation, only the number of the page in the source from which the quotation is taken appears in the parenthetical citation.

> Frank Abagnale has written: "People replace computers with great regularity . . . and their hard drives are crowded with tax returns, bank statements and who knows what else. A woman dumped her old computer on the curb for the garbage collector. It contained

> years of business records. . . . A thief beat the trash man to it and stole her identity" (117).

3. DIRECT QUOTATION WITHOUT MENTIONING THE AUTHOR'S LAST NAME IN THE TEXT OF YOUR PAPER You can introduce a direct quotation without mentioning the author's name in the text of your paper. In that case, put the author's last name and the page from which the quotation was taken in parentheses at the end, just as you would do if you had paraphrased the author's words.

> According to one expert, "One of the saddest aspects of identity theft is that it is often the handiwork of family members—demonstrable evidence that a drastic breakdown in values has poisoned modern society" (Abagnale 80).

Note that even though the author's last name does not appear in the text of the paper, the quotation can still be introduced by a signal phrase: "According to one expert."

4. DIRECT QUOTATION AS PART OF YOUR OWN SENTENCE If you want to make a direct quotation part of your own sentence, quotation marks are the only punctuation marks you need. Just combine the quoted passage with your own words naturally, as in the following sentence. But don't forget the quotation marks.

> At a recent computer security convention held in Las Vegas, "two security consultants showed a room full of hackers, FBI agents and computer security experts how with only $6 and a few lines of code, they could knock out a company's website for a full two hours" (Pacella 68).

Note: When quoting a source, capitalize the first word of a quoted sentence, but do not capitalize the first word of a quoted phrase, especially if you are using the quotation as part of your own sentence.

5. DIRECT QUOTATION OF MORE THAN FOUR LINES If you are including a direct quotation of more than four lines, you must double space it and indent it one half inch from the left margin (called a **block quotation**). No quotation marks are used because the indentation tells your reader that you are quoting directly from a source, as in the following example.

As Bocij points out, there are many ways by which criminals can use the Internet to defraud or damage others:

> At one level a seller might misrepresent an item in an online auction in order to cheat a buyer out of a few extra dollars. At another, a carefully managed stock fraud can damage an entire industry, resulting in losses that can be measured in billions of dollars. Online fraud also ruins the lives of some victims. Fake adoption agencies and dating agencies can cause emotional harm that damages relationships or leads to problems such as depression. Stock fraud can wipe out people's life savings, leaving their future plans, such as retirement, in chaos. (109)

Note that when you use a block quotation, the parenthetical citation goes after the punctuation mark that ends the quotation.

6. SOURCE WITH NO AUTHOR GIVEN If no author's name appears in the source from which you took information, place the title of the source in the parentheses; follow the title with the page number. The source will appear in your works-cited list in alphabetical order by its title.

> "More than 5 million online U.S. households experienced some type of abuse on Facebook in the past year [2010], including virus infections, identity theft, and for a million children, bullying, a *Consumer Reports* survey shows" ("Online Exposure").

The writer has identified the "past year" as 2010 in brackets. No page number is indicated because the source is not paginated.

7. INDIRECT SOURCE When using material quoted in your source, type *qtd. in*, for "quoted in," before your source's name in the parenthetical citation.

> According to Weimann, "all active terrorist groups have established their presence on the Internet" (qtd. in Bocij 17).

8. SELECTION IN AN ANTHOLOGY When referencing the material in such a selection, use the name of the selection's author, not the name of the anthology's editor.

> In "Visionaries, Hucksters, and Con Men," James Surowiecki writes: "One of the striking things about the most recent wave of corporate fraud and deception is how much of it was not centered on Wall Street" (3).

9. TWO OR MORE WORKS BY THE SAME AUTHOR If you are using two or more works by the same author, introduce the material by including the author's name in your signal phrase. Then write the name of the work—in an abbreviated form, if necessary—in the parenthetical citation, along with the page number. An abbreviated title should include only the first noun or noun phrase in the title, without any articles (*a*, *an*, or *the*).

> Paul Bocij claims that "estimates of the number of cyberstalking victims can vary widely." In the United States, for example, they "range from one million to ten million" (*Cyberstalking* 47).

> In his in-depth study of Internet crime, Paul Bocij tells us that "some cyberstalkers attempt to escape blame for their actions by falsely claiming that their victims have harassed them" (*Dark Side* 160).

If you must include both the author and the title in the parenthetical citation, it should look like this:

> One of the telltale signs of cyberstalking is that the culprit expresses an unusually strong and prolonged interest in beginning a close personal relationship with the victim (Bocij, *Dark Side* 164).

10. SOURCE BY TWO AUTHORS If your source has two authors, give the last names of both authors in your signal phrase or parenthetical citation.

> In *Sex, Laws, and Cyberspace*, Wallace and Mangan pose a number of questions relating to regulation of the Internet: "What is the significance of the Net for free speech? Is the Internet

pervasive in the same way as radio and television? What is the role of paternal supervision in determining what children can see on the Net?" (233).

11. SOURCE BY THREE OR MORE AUTHORS With a source that has three or more authors, give only the first author's last name followed by *et al.* (meaning "and others"—with no punctuation between the name and *et al.*) in the signal phrase or parenthetical citation.

> According to the authors, "Most Internet-initiated sex crimes involve adult men who use the Internet to meet and seduce . . . adolescents into sexual encounters" (Wolak et al. 112).

12. THE BIBLE AND OTHER SACRED TEXTS It is not necessary to italicize the words Bible, Talmud, Koran, or other general titles of sacred books, but do italicize specialized editions of those works. Indicate the edition, the book, and the chapter and verse number(s) when you are referencing the Bible. You can do so in the body of the text or in a parenthetical citation. You can abbreviate chapters of the Bible when necessary in the parenthetical citation.

> The end of the flood is explained in the Bible in a way no modern meteorologist would dare: ". . . God made a wind pass over the earth, and the waters assuaged. The fountains also of the deep and the windows of heaven were stopped . . ." (*King James Bible*, Gen. 8.1-2).

13. CORPORATE AUTHOR If authorship is claimed by an organization, you can either use the name of the organization to introduce the information or include its name in the parenthetical citation.

> A virus is defined as "a piece of code or program designed to cause damage to a computer system (by erasing or corrupting data) or to annoy users (by printing messages or altering what is displayed on the computer screen)" (Visual Steps, Inc. 246).

Note that it is appropriate to shorten words that are commonly abbreviated, such as "Inc."

14. IDEAS FROM AN ENTIRE WORK To include information from an entire work, simply include the name(s) of the author(s) in the text or in the parenthetical citation. Obviously, no page number(s) can be indicated.

> Having one's identity stolen can be a harrowing experience, but victims can reclaim their identities by following a few steps recommended by most identity theft crime fighters (Hammond).

15. SOURCE THAT IS NOT PAGINATED You might run across a source that is not paginated, particularly when you are working with online or electronic sources. When page numbers are not available, simply cite the work in its entirety by using the author's last name (if an author is indicated), by using the title, or by using both. If the material is divided into numbered sections or paragraphs, also include these in your parenthetical citation, but only if the sections or paragraphs are stable and would be the same for any reader.

> In an article entitled "Should You Buy ID Theft Protection?" Kimberly Lankford explains that most "theft-monitoring services" will not be able to tell that a Social Security number has been stolen until the thief uses it to apply for a loan or a credit card in the victim's name. However, most identity frauds involve the use of credit-card and bank-account numbers, not Social Security numbers (pars. 2-3).

In the example above, the writer mentions the title of the article ("Should You Buy ID Theft Protection?"), names the author, and then follows up with a parenthetical citation that includes the paragraphs (pars. 2-3) from which this information was summarized.

16. TWO DIFFERENT AUTHORS WITH THE SAME LAST NAME If you cite material by two authors with the same last name, include the first name's initial as well as the last name. If the authors have the same first initial, use the full first name.

> We know that "because identity theft is now part . . . of a slew of other crimes . . . and terrorist attacks, the stakes have risen immeasurably. Involvement, even peripherally, can be deadly" (Robert Hammond 41).

17. INFORMATION FROM TWO DIFFERENT WORKS IN THE SAME SENTENCE Use a semicolon to separate the author and page number(s) of each work in the parenthetical citation.

> According to most experts, one of the most important steps in protecting your identity is not to reveal your Social Security number unless you have to. For example, your employer or your bank may require that information, but an online merchant or someone taking a telephone poll has no business asking you for it (Abagnale 108; Holtzman 6).

18. SOURCE WHOSE AUTHOR IS UNKNOWN If the author's name is not available, you may either use the title of the work to introduce the information or include the title in the parenthetical citation. If you choose the latter option, you can shorten the title to its initial noun or noun phrase, excluding *a*, *an*, or *the*.

> The FBI reports that Americans have become more vulnerable to Internet fraud than ever. The most common complaints to the Bureau concerned online auctions, such as those on eBay; check fraud; investment scams; and "Nigerian email rope-a-dopes" ("Cyber Suckers" 28).

19. MULTIVOLUME WORK If you take information from more than one volume in a multivolume work, indicate the volume number you used in the parenthetical citation. Separate the volume and page number(s) with a colon.

> In *A History of Philosophy*, Frederick Copleston explains that the British chemist and physicist Michael Faraday (1791-1867) became interested in science while he was apprenticed to a bookbinder (8: 18).

However, if you cite only one volume of a multivolume work, you need not include the volume number in your parenthetical citation. In the parenthetical citation, simply state the author's last name followed by the page number, and include the volume number in your works-cited entry.

> *A History of Philosophy* discusses the scientific theories and discoveries of Michael Faraday (Copleston 251).

20. ENCYCLOPEDIA OR DICTIONARY ENTRY When referencing an encyclopedia or dictionary entry, use the entry word itself in the parenthetical reference, not the title (or author, if there is one) of the reference work.

> *Cybernetics* is the science of control systems and "was coined by Norbert Wiener, an American mathematician of the twentieth century" ("Cybernetics").

21. LITERARY WORK If the editions of a literary work are numerous, your works-cited list will tell your reader which edition you are using. You will normally reference a prose work by page number. If you are referencing a play, use act, scene, and line numbers (using Arabic, not Roman, numerals). If you are referencing a poem, reference the part (if the poem is divided into parts) and line numbers (again, in Arabic numerals).

> Early in the play, Lear announces his purpose:
>> Give me the map there. Know that we have divided
>> In three our kingdom; and 'tis our fast intent
>> To shake all cares and business from our age,
>> Conferring them on younger strengths, while we
>> Unburdened crawl toward death. (Lr. 1.1.36-40)

> At the end of *Paradise Lost*, Milton describes the exit of our "first parents" from the Garden of Eden in very poignant lines: "They hand in hand with wandering steps and slow / Through Eden took their solitary way" (12.648-49).

If the poem is not divided into parts, use line numbers. For the first reference, use the word *lines* to let the reader know to what you are referring, such as (lines 72-83). After that, use just the numbers, such as (91-94).

Note: Use Arabic numerals, and separate them with periods only, no space. The titles of works by William Shakespeare can be abbreviated, as shown here.

22. QUOTATION TO WHICH YOU HAVE ADDED MATERIAL OR FROM WHICH YOU HAVE DELETED MATERIAL If you insert something into a direct quotation for whatever reason, put the inserted material in brackets ([ ]). If you delete something from the quoted material, indicate it by using ellipsis points (three spaced periods).

As Holtzman points out,

> the world . . . today is flooded with personal information. Your efforts to protect your data may often seem futile . . . but this doesn't mean you're helpless. Fraud made possible by identity theft may come from every direction, but with few exceptions it always moves toward the same target—your financial assets [bank accounts, credit/debit cards, and investment accounts]. So, even though you can't control inadvertent data breaches . . . you can protect yourself by carefully monitoring your credit history and other financial information. (44)

Use notes with parenthetical documentation as necessary.

You may use two kinds of notes in addition to parenthetical documentation: (1) notes that provide the reader with information, explanations, and comments that cannot be included in the text, and (2) bibliographic notes that list other sources or provide evaluative comments.

To indicate these notes, place a superscript Arabic numeral at the appropriate place in your text and write the information after a matching numeral either at the bottom of the page (a footnote) or at the end of the text (an endnote).

MLA Style for Works-Cited Entries

A works-cited list, at the very end of your paper, is an *alphabetical list* of all the sources—books, articles, book reviews, interviews, and so on—from which you obtained the information you used in your paper. It lists complete publication information about each source referenced in your paper's parenthetical citations. Although the format of the individual entries (sources) in a works-cited list and the information they supply vary according to the type of source, the list as a whole is arranged in the pattern described below.

1. Entries are listed alphabetically by the last name of the author or by the first major word of the title if no author is given. If a source has more than one author, it is alphabetized by the last name of the author whose name appears first. The entries are not numbered.

2. Entries are double-spaced.

3. The first line of each entry begins at the left margin. If more than one line is needed to complete the entry, additional lines are indented half an inch (this is called a **hanging indent**).

Note: An *annotated bibliography* is a list of sources used in a research paper that includes, for each entry, an explanatory note identifying the focus of the information and providing a brief description or evaluation of the source.

The exact information you include for each source in your works-cited list depends on the source. Thus, a works-cited-list entry for a book is different from an entry for a magazine or journal article, and both are different from an entry for an electronic source. You can use the following sample entries as models for those in your own list of works cited. (You should refer to these samples when you write bibliography cards as well, because doing so will save you time when you compose your works-cited list.)

Note that in 2016, the Modern Language Association made several changes to the style used in a works-cited list, including these:

- Do not include the publication medium such as "Print" or "Web."
- Include URLs in Web entries, unless instructed otherwise.
- Use the abbreviations "vol." and "no." to indicate the volume and issue number of a periodical.
- Use "p." or "pp." for "page" or "pages."
- Spell out "editor," "translator," and similar words.
- Use a period after author name and after title; use commas after other elements.
- Include only if useful to the reader or important to your project the following information: city of publisher, year of original publication, date of access for a Web source.

Books

1. BOOK BY A SINGLE AUTHOR

Abagnale, Frank. *Stealing Your Life*. Broadway Books, 2007.

Elements of the Preceding Entry

Abagnale, Frank. The author's name (last name first), followed by a period.

Stealing Your Life. The title of the book in italics, followed by a period.

11

> **Broadway Books, 2007.** The publisher of the book, followed by a comma. The year the book was published, followed by a period.

2. BOOK WITH A SUBTITLE, BY A SINGLE AUTHOR

> Bocij, Paul. *The Dark Side of the Internet: Protecting Yourself and Your Family from Online Criminals.* Praeger, 2006.

MLA style calls for shortening a publisher's name as long as doing so does not create confusion or leave out information that the reader will need to identify the publisher. For example, you can shorten *McGraw-Hill Education* to *McGraw-Hill*. Also, you can omit words or abbreviations in the publisher's name, such as "Company" or "Ltd."

3. BOOK BY TWO AUTHORS

> Wallace, Jonathan, and Mark Mangan. *Sex, Love, and Cyberspace: Freedom and Censorship on the Frontiers of the Online Revolution.* Holt, 1996.

4. BOOK BY THREE OR MORE AUTHORS

> Loberg, Kristin, et al. *Identity Theft: How to Protect Your Name, Your Credit, and Your Vital Information . . . and What to Do When Someone Hijacks Any of These.* Silver Lake, 2004.

The Latin abbreviation *et al.* means "and others." It is used in place of the names of all authors except the first when there are three or more authors.

5. BOOK BY AN UNKNOWN AUTHOR If the author's name is not given, begin with the title. Place the book in the list of works cited by alphabetizing according to the first letter of the first major word in the title. The following entry would appear under "C" for "Careers."

> *Careers in Information Technology.* Wet Feet, 2007.

6. TWO OR MORE BOOKS BY THE SAME AUTHOR List the items in alphabetical order according to the first major word in the title. Place the author's name in the first item only. In the item(s) that follow, type three hyphens and a period in place of the author's name:

> Bocij, Paul. *Cyberstalking*. Praeger, 2004.
>
> ---. *The Dark Side of the Internet: Protecting Yourself and Your Family from Online Criminals*. Praeger, 2006.
>
> ---. *Software for Free*. Kuma Publishing, 1992.

7. BOOK WITH AN EDITOR OR EDITORS

> Surowiecki, James, editor. *Best Business Crime Writing of the Year*. Anchor, 2002.

8. BOOK IN A SERIES Type the series name at the end of the entry. Do not italicize or use quotation marks around the name of the series.

> Dickens, Charles. *Great Expectations*. Edited by Janisae Carlisle, Bedford, 1996. Case Studies in Contemporary Criticism 4.

9. BOOK CONTAINING THE TITLE OF ANOTHER WORK WITHIN ITS TITLE If the title of another work appears within the title of the book you are citing, ask yourself whether that other work would be in italics if it stood alone. If the answer is yes, *do not* italicize it.

> Alexander, Nigel. *Poison, Play, and Duel: A Study in* Hamlet. U of Nebraska P, 1971.

The abbreviations *U* and *P* stand for "University" and "Press."

On the other hand, if the title of that other work would appear in quotation marks if it stood alone, place quotation marks around it and italicize the entire title of the book in which the other title appears.

> Patrides, C. A., editor. *"Lycidas": The Tradition and the Poem*. Holt, 1961.

10. EDITION OTHER THAN THE FIRST

If you are listing a work that has been republished in a later edition or editions, indicate the number of the edition you are using.

> Modern Language Association, *MLA Handbook*. 8th ed., MLA, 2016.

11. MULTIVOLUME WORK

> Durant, Will, and Ariel Durant. *The Story of Civilization*. Simon and Schuster, 1935-75. 11 vols.

If your paper cites only one of the volumes, indicate the volume number before the publisher and note the number of volumes in the work after the date if that information will help your reader find the source:

> Durant, Will. *The Life of Greece*. 1939. *The Story of Civilization*, vol. 2, Simon and Schuster, 1935-75.

> Anderson, Theodore, and Mildred Boyer. *Bilingual Schooling in the United States*. Vol. 1, Government Printing Office, 1970. 11 vols.

12. SELECTION FROM AN ANTHOLOGY

> Griggs, Brandon. "The 12 Most Annoying Types of Facebookers." 2010. *75 Readings Plus*, edited by Santi V. Buscemi and Charlotte Smith, 10th ed., McGraw-Hill, 2013, pp. 187-92.

If the selection in the anthology was previously published, you may give the date when the selection first appeared by placing it after the title, followed by a period.

13. ANTHOLOGY WITH AN EMPHASIS ON THE EDITOR OR EDITORS

> Buscemi, Santi V., and Charlotte Smith, editors. *75 Readings Plus*. 10th ed., McGraw-Hill, 2013.

14. TWO OR MORE SELECTIONS FROM THE SAME ANTHOLOGY In one entry, give full publication information for the anthology. In addition, list each selection separately with the name(s) of the author(s) and the title of the selection in quotation marks, followed by the last name(s) of the anthology's editor(s), followed by the page numbers on which the selection appears.

> Baldwin, James. "Fifth Avenue, Uptown." Buscemi and Smith,
>
> pp. 49-53.
>
> Buscemi, Santi V., and Charlotte Smith, editors. *75 Readings Plus*.
>
> 10th ed., McGraw-Hill, 2013.
>
> Casey, Susan. "Our Oceans Are Turning into Plastic: Are We?"
>
> Buscemi and Smith, pp. 314-24.

15. TRANSLATION—FOCUS ON THE ORIGINAL AUTHOR Begin with the author's name (last name first). Follow with the title, the translator's name, and the publication information.

> Barthes, Roland. *The Fashion System*. Translated by Matthew
>
> Ward and Richard Howard, U of California P, 1990.

16. TRANSLATION—FOCUS ON THE TRANSLATOR Begin with the name(s) of the translator(s). Follow with the title, the author's name, and the publication information.

> Ward, Matthew, and Richard Howard, translators. *The Fashion*
>
> *System*. By Roland Barthes, U of California P, 1990.

17. FOREWORD, INTRODUCTION, PREFACE, AFTERWORD, OR EPILOGUE Include the name of the section after the author. End with a period.

> Alatis, James E., et al. Introduction. *Linguistics, Language*
>
> *Acquisition, and Language Variation: Current Trends and*
>
> *Future Projects*, Georgetown UP, 1996, pp. 1-2.
>
> Javers, Eamon. Epilogue. *Broker, Trader, Lawyer, Spy: The Secret*
>
> *World of Corporate Espionage*. By Javers, HarperCollins,
>
> 2010, pp. 275-77.

18. BOOK PUBLISHED BY AN ORGANIZATION OR A CORPORATION
List the corporate author first, followed by the title. Then list the publisher. If the author and the publisher are the same, put the title at the beginning and list the corporate author as the publisher.

> Wings of Success. *Identity Theft—Don't Be the Next Victim.* Prime Books, 2010.

19. REPUBLISHED BOOK When citing a republished book—for example, a paperback version of a book originally published in a hardcover version—the original publication date is optional. However, if the original date would be useful for the reader, include it, followed by a period, before the publication information for the book you are citing.

> Zentalla, Ana Celia. *Growing Up Bilingual: Puerto Rican Children in New York.* 1997. Blackwell, 2000.

20. ENCYCLOPEDIA OR DICTIONARY

> "Artificial Intelligence." *McGraw-Hill Encyclopedia of Science & Technology.* 10th ed., 2007.

> "Godiva, Lady." *Dictionary of Cultural Literacy*, 2nd ed., Houghton Mifflin, 1993, p. 199.

If the article is signed, begin the entry with the author's name, last name first.

21. BIBLE OR OTHER SACRED TEXT

> *Holy Bible.* King James Version. Nelson, 1976.

Articles printed in periodicals
22. ARTICLE IN A MAGAZINE—SIGNED AND UNSIGNED

Signed

> Mediati, Nick. "Secure Your Life in 12 Steps: Learn to Lock Down Your Computer, Your Home Network, Your Identity—Even Your Phone." *PC World*, June 2011, pp. 59-66.

Elements of the Preceding Entry

Mediati, Nick.	The author's name (last name first), followed by a period.
"Secure Your Life in 12 Steps: Learn to Lock Down Your Computer, Your Home Network, Your Identity—Even Your Phone."	The title of the article in quotation marks, followed by a period within the closing quotation mark.
PC World,	The title of the magazine in italics, followed by a comma.
June 2011,	The date of publication, followed by a comma.
pp. 59-66.	The pages of the magazine on which the article appears, followed by a period. Use "p." for one page and "pp." for multiple pages.

Unsigned

"Cyber Suckers." *Atlantic Monthly,* July-Aug., 2008, p. 28.

23. ARTICLE IN A SCHOLARLY JOURNAL, PAGINATED BY VOLUME

Anderson, Keith B., et al. "Identity Theft." J*ournal of Economic Perspectives,* vol. 22, no. 2, 2008, pp. 171-92.

Generally, libraries bind all the issues of a volume together if the page numbers run consecutively, starting with the first and ending with the last. In such cases, no issue needs to be indicated, as in the following example.

Spafford, Eugene. "Protecting the Internet from the Criminal Element." *Science News*, vol. 174, 2008, p. 32.

24. ARTICLE IN A SCHOLARLY JOURNAL, PAGINATED BY ISSUE

> Morris-Cotterill, Nigel. "Money Laundering." *Foreign Policy*, no. 124, 2001, pp. 16-23.

Note that only the issue number is available for the above item. However, include both the volume number and the issue number if both are available.

25. ARTICLE IN A SCHOLARLY JOURNAL, BY MULTIPLE AUTHORS

> Borenstein, Severin, and Garth Saloner. "Economics and Electronic Commerce." *Journal of Economic Perspectives*, vol. 15, no. 1, 2001, pp. 3-12.

> Wolak, Janis, et al. "Online 'Predators' and Their Victims: Myths, Realities, and Implications for Prevention and Treatment." *American Psychologist*, vol. 63, no. 2, 2008, pp. 111-28.

26. ARTICLE IN A NEWSPAPER—SIGNED AND UNSIGNED

Signed

> Mossberg, Walter S. "How to Avoid Cons That Can Lead to Identity Theft." *The Wall Street Journal*, 1 May 2008, pp. D1-D2.

For daily newspapers, the date (given as day, month, year) replaces the volume and issue number. You may need to supply section numbers or letters in addition to page numbers. If the newspaper is not widely known, you should include the city in which it is published unless the city appears in the title. Thus, if you were citing the *Star Ledger*, which is published in Newark, New Jersey, you would write *Star Ledger* [Newark, NJ].

Unsigned

> "Police Warning in Fight against Internet Crime." *Leicester Mercury*, 3 Aug. 2007, p. 5.

27. EDITORIAL IN A NEWSPAPER Use the same format for an editorial as for an unsigned article, but type the word *Editorial* immediately after the title of the editorial.

"Keeping Personal Data Private." Editorial. *The New York Times*, 25 Nov. 2009, p. A30.

28. LETTER TO THE EDITOR

Wyman, L. W. "My Social Security Number." Letter. *The New York Times*, 7 Dec. 2010, p. 34.

29. BOOK REVIEW

Yagoda, Ben. "Slow Down, Sign Off, Tune Out." Review of *The Tyranny of E-Mail* by John Freeman. *The New York Times Book Review*, 25 Oct. 2009, p. 9.

Note that in this item, the title of the review differs from the title of the work reviewed. In some short reviews, however, the title of the review and that of the work can be identical.

Digital sources

Because works published in digital media are not as fixed and stable as print works, they require more citation information than references to printed documents. Often, however, digital sources do not supply all the needed information, such as page or paragraph numbers, so you just have to cite whatever information you can find. Many times, for instance, an online document will not have been published in a print version; obviously, in that case, you cannot include information about the print publication. The following example of a common type of citation (an article in an online publication) shows all the information you *should* include in a citation if the information is available.

30. ARTICLE IN AN ONLINE PUBLICATION

Castillo, Michelle. "NY Senator: HTTP 'a Welcome Mat for Would-Be Hackers.'" *Time.com*, 28 Feb. 2011, techland.time.com/2011/02/28/ ny-senator-http-a-welcome-mat-for-would-be-hackers/.

Elements of the Preceding Entry

Castillo, Michelle.	The author's name (last name first), followed by a period. If there is no author's name, begin the entry with the title of the article.
"NY Senator: HTTP 'a Welcome Mat for Would-Be Hackers.' "	The title of the article in quotation marks, followed by a period within the closing quotation marks.
Time.com,	The title of the online publication in italics, followed by a comma.
28 Feb. 2011,	The date of electronic publication, followed by a comma.
techland.time.com/2011/02/28/ny-senator-http-a-welcome-mat-for-would-be-hackers/.	The URL (without "http://"), followed by a period.

31. ARTICLE OR DOCUMENT ON AN INTERNET SITE WITH SOME INFORMATION MISSING

"Smokeless Tobacco Is Addictive." *Truth*, n.d., www.thetruth.com/the-facts/fact-208.

Elements of the Preceding Entry

"Smokeless Tobacco Is Addictive."	When the document has no author, start with the title of the article or document in quotation marks, ending with a period inside the closing quotation mark.
Truth,	The title of the Internet site in italics, followed by a comma.

n.d.,	The date on which the article or document was posted or last revised. If no date can be found, write *n.d.* for "no date." End with a comma.
www.thetruth.com/the-facts/fact-208.	The URL, followed by a period.

Note: The date of access for any electronic source is an optional element, but if the date is important for readers because it indicates which version you used and/or is the only date available, include it at the end of the citation, starting with the word *Accessed*.

"Smokeless Tobacco Is Addictive." *Truth*, n.d., www.thetruth.com/

the-facts/fact-208. Accessed 23 Mar. 2015.

32. HOME PAGE FOR A COURSE OR AN ACADEMIC DEPARTMENT
Begin the entry with the name of the course instructor (last name first); then list the title of the course followed by the description "Course home page" or "Home page" (but not italicized or in quotation marks). Include the date of the page, the names of the department and/or institution, and the URL.

Thomas, Diane. World Literature II (English 252). Course home

page, Spring 2011, English Department, Northern Virginia

Community College, novaonline.nvcc.edu/eli/eng252/

eng252courseguide.htm.

Department of Chemistry. Home page, 2016, Virginia Tech,

www.chem.vt.edu/.

33. ONLINE BOOK
Follow the directions for citing a printed book, modifying them where necessary for an electronic source. For example, you may need to add the electronic publication information, date of electronic publication, and date of access.

Anderson, Sherwood. *Winesburg, Ohio*. 1919. *Great Books Online*,

www.bartleby.com/156/index.html.

Note that the original publication date is an optional item; include it if your reader will find it useful, such as if historical context is needed.

34. PART OF AN ONLINE BOOK

Dickinson, Emily. "Success is counted sweetest." *The Complete Poems*, *Great Books Online*, www.bartleby.com/113/1001.html.

Place the title of the part or chapter in quotation marks. Place the title of the book in italics. Next, provide the name of the Web site (in italics) on which the book can be found, followed by the URL.

35. ARTICLE IN AN ONLINE SCHOLARLY JOURNAL

Peterson, Bob. "Leaving English Learners Behind." *Rethinking Schools*, vol. 16, no. 3, 2003, www.rethinkingschools.org/special_reports/bilingual/leav171.shtml.

Scholarly journals can be found online independently (as in the example above) or as part of an academic database. If you are citing a journal that is part of a database, use the model listed in item 43.

36. ARTICLE IN AN ONLINE NEWSPAPER OR FROM A NEWSWIRE

Steinberg, Jacques. "Answers to an English Question." *The New York Times*, 22 Oct. 2000, www.nytimes.com/2000/10/22/nyregion/answers-english-question-instead-ending-program-new-york-may-offer-choice.html.

37. ONLINE REVIEW

Henry, Peter. "Phishing: Cutting the Identity Theft Line." Review of *Phishing: Cutting the Identity Theft Line*, by Rachel Lininger and Russell Dean Vines. *Journal of Digital Forensic Practice*, vol. 1, no. 3, 24 Feb. 2007, doi:10.1080/15567280601047492.

In this case, the title of the review is the same as the title of the book being reviewed. Frequently, however, the author of the review will use a title different from that of the work reviewed. Also note that a digital object identifier (DOI) is used, rather than a URL. Always use a DOI or a permalink (stable URL) if it is available.

38. ARTICLE IN AN ONLINE MAGAZINE

Bennett, Robert. "Internet Fraud and Online Scams." *Suite 101*, 27 Apr. 2010, www.suite101.com/bennett/internet_fraud.html.

39. ANONYMOUS ARTICLE IN AN ONLINE MAGAZINE

"Save the Internet by Doing Nothing." *Slate.com*, 20 July 2009, www.slate.com/articles/technology/future_tense/2011/01/save_the_internet_by_doing_nothing.html.

40. EDITORIAL IN AN ONLINE PUBLICATION

"Bill Raises Risk of Identity Theft." Editorial. *Sun Journal* [Lewiston/Auburn], 22 Sept. 2011, www.sunjournal.com/articles/bill_raises_risk_of_identity_theft.html.

41. LETTER TO THE EDITOR (ONLINE)

Kozak, Kris. "Identifying Victims of ID Theft." Letter. *Kansas City Star.com*, 26 Apr. 2008, www.kansascitystar.com/kozak/identifying.htm.

42. NONPERIODICAL PUBLICATION ON CD-ROM, DISKETTE, OR MAGNETIC TAPE
This source should be cited the same way you would cite a book source, but with an indication of the medium of publication (*CD-ROM, Diskette, Magnetic tape,* not italicized). Usually, only one publication date and one vendor's name are given because the information provider and publisher are almost always the same for this type of source.

"Cybernetics." *McGraw-Hill Encyclopedia of Science and Technology.* McGraw-Hill, 1999. CD-ROM.

43. ARTICLE FROM A PROFESSIONAL JOURNAL, NEWSPAPER, OR MAGAZINE FOUND IN AN ACADEMIC DATABASE In each case, create an entry for the printed version of the article. Follow that with the name of the database and the URL. The example below is for an article from a magazine.

> Leggiere, Michael V. "From Berlin to Leipzig: Napoleon's Gamble in North Germany, 1813." *The Journal of Military History*, vol. 67, no. 1, Jan. 2003, pp. 39-84. *JSTOR*, www.jstor.org/stable/3093168.

44. E-MAIL OR TEXT

> Saunders, Nicholas. "Re: Questionnaire for Doctoral Dissertation." Received by the Author. 10 Feb. 2011.

45. BLOG POSTING

> Dunphy, Chris. "Can You Stay in 55+ RV Parks If You're under 55?" *Technomadia*, 17 Mar. 2016, www.technomadia.com/2016/03/can-you-stay-in-55-rv-parks-if-youre-under-55/.

46. TWEET Include the entire tweet as the title. Include the word *Twitter* (in italics), the date and time sent, and the URL.

> @spincaster. "The candidates are beginning to arrive on stage at the Civic Center." *Twitter*, 18 Apr. 2016, 4:25 p.m., twitter.com/spincaster//38273433.

Other sources: print and nonprint (including digital versions)

This section includes examples of traditional print sources, as well as multimedia sources not covered elsewhere in this chapter. If you find one of the sources in this section online, follow the model for that source, giving whatever additional information is available for the online source.

47. ADVERTISEMENT When citing an advertisement, give the name of the product, company, or institution. Follow it with the word *Advertisement* (not in quotation marks or italics). Finish the citation with the usual publication information.

> Cartier. Advertisement. *Vanity Fair*, May 2000, p. 45.

48. CARTOON OR COMIC STRIP State the name of the cartoonist or comic strip artist. Follow the name with the title of the cartoon or comic strip (if any), in quotation marks, and the word *Cartoon* or the words *Comic strip* (not in quotation marks or italics). Finish the citation with the usual publication information.

> Donnelly, Liza. "This Place Reeks of Education." Cartoon. *New*
>
> *Yorker*, 26 Sept. 1994, p. 72.
>
> Johnston, Lynn. "For Better or for Worse." Comic strip.
>
> *Star-Ledger* [Newark], 16 April 2002, p. 44.

With names of newspapers that might not be known to some readers, add the place of publication in brackets.

49. DISSERTATION—ABSTRACT Begin with the author's name, followed by the title of the dissertation in quotation marks. Then type the word *Dissertation* (not italicized) and the name of the university at which the dissertation was written, followed by the date of its completion. End with the abbreviation *DA* or *DAI* (for *Dissertation Abstracts* or *Dissertation Abstracts International)*, followed by the volume, the year of publication, and the page number.

> Raymond, Albert J. "Relationships among Bilingualism, Critical
>
> Thinking Ability, and Critical Thinking Disposition of
>
> Baccalaureate Nursing Students." Dissertation, U of
>
> Florida, 1996, *DAI*, vol. 58/07, 1997, p. 2526.

50. DISSERTATION—PUBLISHED Treat a published dissertation as a book. However, add the word *Dissertation* (not italicized) after the title, as well as the name of the university that granted the doctorate and the year the dissertation was completed. End with the publication information as usual.

> Murphy-Shigematsu, Steven. *The Voices of Ameriasians.*
>
> Dissertation. Harvard U, 1986. Dissertations.com, 2000.

To cite a master's thesis, substitute *MA thesis* or *MS thesis* for *Dissertation*.

51. DISSERTATION—UNPUBLISHED Begin with the author's name, followed by the title of the dissertation, in quotation marks. Then type the word *Dissertation* (not italicized), as well as the name of the university that granted the doctorate and the year in which the dissertation was completed.

> Dann, Emily. "An Experimental Pre-Statistics Curriculum for Two-Year College Students." Dissertation, Rutgers U, 1976.

52. GOVERNMENT PUBLICATION Ordinarily, the government (whether federal, state, or municipal) is considered the author of such works. After typing the name of the government, type the name of the specific agency that published the work, if known. Also include any optional information relevant to your paper.

> United States, Congress, House, Committee on Homeland Security. *Secure Our Borders First Act of 2015*. Government Printing Office, 2015. 114th Congress, 1st session, House Report 114-10.

53. LECTURE OR ADDRESS Begin with the speaker's name, followed by the title of the presentation in quotation marks and the name of the sponsoring organization. End with the place and date of the presentation and the descriptive label *Lecture* or *Address* (not italicized).

> Da Rienzo, William. "The Need for Computer Security." The American Association for Identity-Theft Protection, Nashville, TN, 9 Feb. 2011. Lecture.

54. PLAY—LIVE PERFORMANCE Begin with the title of the play, followed by the name of its author. Next, indicate the names of the director and the principal performers. End with the name of the theater, its location, the date of the performance you saw, and a descriptive label, if necessary.

> *The Iceman Cometh*. By Eugene O'Neill. Directed by Howard Davies, performance by Kevin Spacey and Tony Danza. Brooks Atkinson Theater, New York, 22 June 1999. Performance.

55. MAP OR CHART When citing a map or chart, treat it as you would an anonymous book, but add the label *Map* or *Chart* (not italicized).

> *The Inca: An Empire and Its Ancestors*. Map, National Geographic, 2002.

56. MOTION PICTURE If it is relevant, include the original date the film was released following the title.

>   *Grand Hotel*. 1932. Directed by Edmund Goulding, performance by Greta Garbo, John Barrymore, Joan Crawford, Wallace Beery, and Lionel Barrymore, Warner Home Video, 2013.

57. PAMPHLET As with a book, begin the entry with the author's name, if known. If the author is unknown, begin with the title of the pamphlet.

>   Burr, William E., et al. *Electronic Authentication Guideline: Information Technology*. National Institute of Standards and Technology, 2006.

58. PERSONAL INTERVIEW

>   Kelly, James, Personal interview, 17 Jan. 2011.

59. PERSONAL LETTER Begin with the writer's name, followed by *Letter to the author* (not italicized) and the date.

>   Cornell, Molly. Letter to the author. 11 Sept. 2008.

60. PUBLISHED INTERVIEW Begin with the name of the person interviewed. Follow with the title of the interview, if any, in quotation marks. If the title of the interview does not include the word *Interview* or if the interview has no title, simply type the word *Interview* (not italicized) after the subject's name.

>   Gates, Bill. "One-on-One with Bill Gates." Interview by Kevin Chapell, *Ebony*, Oct. 2011, p. 83.

61. RADIO OR TELEVISION INTERVIEW Begin with the name of the person interviewed, followed by the word *Interview* (not italicized). Then include the title of the program (italicized). End with the name of the network and the date on which the program was aired.

>   Gates, Bill. Interview. *American Morning*, CNN, 13 June 2011.

62. RADIO OR TELEVISION PROGRAM If you are drawing information from a titled episode of a program, begin with the title of that episode, in quotation marks. If not, begin with the name of the program (italicized). Then indicate any descriptive label relevant to your paper, such as the name of the host, narrator, director, creator, or performer. Next, type the season number (if available), episode number (if available), production company, and year of broadcast. Start the citation with the item that is most relevant to your paper and that you cited within the paper.

> "The Great Chain." *The American Revolution*, hosted by William Curtis, History Channel, 3 July 1999.

> "Hounded." *Elementary*, performance by Jonny Lee Miller and Lucy Liu, season 4, episode 16, CBS, 10 Mar. 2016.

63. SONG LYRICS

> Midler, Bette, and Marc Shaiman. "Nobody Else But You." *Bette*, Warner Brothers, 2000.

64. SOUND RECORDING OR MUSIC FROM AN ALBUM

> Verdi, Giuseppe. *La Traviata*. Performance by Ileana Cotrubas, Placido Domingo, and Sherrill Milnes, Deutsche Grammophon, 1977, itunes.apple.com/us/album/verdi-la-traviata/id920267429.

Note: Include the URL if the lyrics or sound recording is on the Web.

65. LEGAL OR HISTORICAL DOCUMENT With public questions, propositions, or referenda, provide the author; the title of the question, proposition, or referendum; the date it was proposed; and the URL if the source was electronic.

> California, Office of the Attorney General. *Proposition 227: English Language in the Public Schools*, Nov. 1998.

With legal decisions, provide title and number of the decision, the name of the court that issued the decision, and the date it was announced.

> Brown v. Board of Education of Topeka. No. 347-483. Supreme Court of the United States, 17 May 1954.

66. DVD Use the same format you would use for a video source, but include the disc number at the end. As with any performance source, include whatever relevant information is needed, such as name of director, writer, or performer.

> "Part Two: Perestroika." *Angels in America*, directed by Mike Nichols, screenplay by Tony Kushner, episode 4, HBO Films, 2004, disc 2.

67. WORK OF ART Begin with the artist's name, if known, followed by the title of the work (italicized), the date the work was completed, and the name of the institution and city where the work is housed.

> Hopper, Edward. *Nighthawks*. 1942, Art Institute, Chicago.

If the source of the work is an image in a book or on a Web site, include the appropriate publication information.

> Hockney, David. *A Bigger Splash*. 1967, Tate Gallery, London. *Sister Wendy's 1000 Masterpieces*, authored by Sister Wendy Beckett, DK, 1999.

Directory of In-Text Citations and Works-Cited Entries

In-Text Citations

1. Summarized or paraphrased material 2
2. Direct quotation with author's last name in the text 2
3. Direct quotation without author's last name in the text 3
4. Direct quotation as part of your own sentence 3
5. Direct quotation of more than four lines 3
6. Source with no author given 4
7. Indirect source 4
8. Selection in an anthology 5
9. Two or more works by the same author 5
10. Source by two authors 5
11. Source by three or more authors 6
12. The Bible and other sacred texts 6
13. Corporate author 6
14. Ideas from an entire work 7
15. Source that is not paginated 7
16. Two different authors with the same last name 7
17. Two works cited in the same sentence 8
18. Source whose author is unknown 8
19. Multivolume work 8
20. Encyclopedia or dictionary entry 9
21. Literary work 9
22. Quotation with material added or deleted 9

Works-Cited Entries

Books

1. Book by a single author 11
2. Book with a subtitle, by a single author 12
3. Book by two authors 12
4. Book by three or more authors 12
5. Book by an unknown author 12
6. Two or more books by the same author 13
7. Book with an editor or editors 13
8. Book in a series 13

9. Book containing the title of another work within its title 13
10. Edition other than the first 14
11. Multivolume work 14
12. Selection from an anthology 14
13. Anthology with an emphasis on the editor or editors 14
14. Two or more selections from the same anthology 15
15. Translation—focus on the original author 15
16. Translation—focus on the translator 15
17. Foreword, introduction, preface, afterword, or epilogue 15
18. Book published by an organization or a corporation 16
19. Republished book 16
20. Encyclopedia or dictionary 16
21. Bible or other sacred text 16

Periodical Articles (Print)
22. Article in a magazine—signed and unsigned 16
23. Article in a scholarly journal, paginated by volume 17
24. Article in a scholarly journal, paginated by issue 18
25. Article in a scholarly journal, by multiple authors 18
26. Article in a newspaper—signed and unsigned 18
27. Editorial in a newspaper 19
28. Letter to the editor 19
29. Book review 19

Digital Sources
30. Article in an online publication 19
31. Article or document on an Internet site with some information missing 20
32. Home page for a course or an academic department 21
33. Online book 21
34. Part of an online book 22
35. Article in an online scholarly journal 22
36. Article in an online newspaper or from a newswire 22
37. Online review 22
38. Article in an online magazine 23
39. Anonymous article in an online magazine 23
40. Editorial in an online publication 23

41. Letter to the editor (online) 23
42. Nonperiodical publication on CD-ROM, diskette, or magnetic tape 23
43. Article from a professional journal, newspaper, or magazine found in an academic database 23
44. E-mail or text 24
45. Blog posting 24
46. Tweet 24

Other Sources: Print and Nonprint (Including Digital Versions)
47. Advertisement 24
48. Cartoon or comic strip 25
49. Dissertation—abstract 25
50. Dissertation—published 25
51. Dissertation—unpublished 25
52. Government publication 26
53. Lecture or address 26
54. Play—live performance 26
55. Map or chart 26
56. Motion picture 27
57. Pamphlet 27
58. Personal interview 27
59. Personal letter 27
60. Published interview 27
61. Radio or television interview 27
62. Radio or television program 28
63. Song lyrics 28
64. Sound recording or music from an album 28
65. Legal or historical document 28
66. DVD 29
67. Work of art 29